The Tastiest Mediterranean Diet for Seniors

Discover How to Lose Weight, Protect Your Heart and Brain with Healthy, Mouthwatering Recipes, and Enjoy a Meal Plan Designed for Adults Over 60

Zoe Makris

Copyright © 2025 by Zoe Makris
All rights reserved.
No part of this book may be reproduced in any form without permission from the publisher or the author, except as permitted by the copyright law of the country in which the book is sold.

CONTENTS

INTRODUCTION.. 1
Chapter 1 – The Traditional Mediterranean Diet vs The Modern Mediterranean Diet. 2
Chapter 2 – Health Benefits for Seniors. 4
Chapter 3 – Nutritious and Easy Breakfasts. 5
3.1 Black Olive and Tomato Whole Grain Focaccia. 5
3.2 Greek Yogurt with Honey and Walnuts. 9
3.3 Bruschetta. 13
3.4 Fresh Seasonal Fruit. 17
3.5 Gluten-Free Fig Olive Oil Cake. 21
Chapter 4 – Balanced Lunches for Energy and Digestion. 25
4.1 Legume and Spelt Soup. 25
4.2 Ensalada de Garbanzos. 29
4.3 Mediterranean Salad Grilled Octopus. 33
4.4 Mediterranean-Style Shrimps. 37
4.5 Pisto Manchego with Egg. 41
Chapter 5 – Light but Flavorful Dinners
 5.1 Psari Plaki (Baked Fish with Tomato). 45
5.2 Moussaka. 49
5.3 Lemon Sardines. 53
5.4 Cuttlefish and Peas. 57
5.5 Baked Sea Bream with Fennel and Lemon. 61
Chapter 6 – Healthy Snacks Throughout the Day
 6.1 Black Olive Tapenade with Crostini 64
6.2 Feta with Cucumber and Oregano. 68
6.3 Mixed Dried Fruit. 72
6.4 Fresh Fruit with Lemon Zest. 77
6.5 Herbal Tea with Spelt and Sesame Cookies. 81
Conclusion. 85
Bibliography. 86

INTRODUCTION

As we grow older, our bodies change—and so do our nutritional needs. Seniors face unique health challenges, from maintaining heart health and cognitive function to supporting bone strength and digestion. Yet, the path to aging well doesn't lie in strict diets or trendy fads. It lies in something much simpler, time-tested, and delicious: the Traditional Mediterranean Diet.

This book was born out of a desire to bring together the best of both worlds—ancient culinary wisdom and modern nutritional science—into a practical, joyful guide tailored specifically for seniors.

The Mediterranean lifestyle is more than just a way of eating. It's a cultural treasure rooted in fresh, seasonal ingredients, mindful eating, and community. Research shows that this way of living can support longevity, reduce the risk of chronic diseases, and improve quality of life—all things that matter even more as we age.

Scan the QR to access the bonus: Greek Sweets

Chapter 1 – The Traditional Mediterranean Diet VS The Modern Mediterranean Diet

Today, the term "Mediterranean diet" is used everywhere–from cookbooks to restaurants to food packaging. But not everything labeled "Mediterranean" reflects the true essence of the traditional lifestyle that gave this diet its reputation for promoting health and longevity.
So, what's the difference?

The Traditional Mediterranean Diet

The traditional version of the Mediterranean diet–practiced from the early 20th century up until the 1960s in rural parts of Italy, Greece, and southern Spain–was simple, seasonal, and deeply connected to the land. People grew their own food, bought from local markets, and cooked at home. Meals were made from scratch using fresh vegetables, legumes, whole grains, olive oil, herbs, and occasionally fish, eggs, or cheese. Meat was rare and eaten mostly on special occasions.

The Modern Mediterranean Diet

Today, many diets inspired by Mediterranean cuisine still include healthy elements, but they've become influenced by Western eating patterns. The modern version—especially in urban areas—often includes:
- More processed foods, snacks, and sweets
- Higher amounts of refined grains and sugars
- Larger portions and more frequent meat consumption
- Less home cooking and more convenience foods
- A shift toward a more sedentary lifestyle

These changes have diluted the benefits of the original Mediterranean lifestyle. In fact, many people living in Mediterranean countries today no longer follow the traditional diet—and rates of chronic diseases like obesity and heart disease have increased as a result.

Why It Matters

Understanding the difference helps us return to the roots of what makes this diet so powerful—especially for seniors. The traditional Mediterranean diet isn't just healthier; it's also more sustainable, affordable, and fulfilling. By embracing its original principles, we can enjoy its full benefits in the modern world.

Scan the QR to access the bonus: 4-week meal plan

Chapter 2 – Health Benefits for Seniors

A Strong Heart and Controlled Blood Pressure
The Traditional Mediterranean Diet helps seniors protect heart health by lowering blood pressure, reducing inflammation, and improving cholesterol levels. Key foods include extra virgin olive oil, fresh fruits and vegetables, legumes, whole grains, and fish. Studies like PREDIMED show it significantly lowers the risk of heart attacks and strokes.

A Sharp Mind and Active Memory
This diet supports brain health with nutrients that reduce inflammation and oxidative stress. Olive oil, vegetables, berries, fish, and whole grains contribute to better memory and slower cognitive decline. It also promotes mindful eating habits that benefit mental well-being.

Daily Energy and Vitality
The diet provides long-lasting energy through complex carbs, healthy fats, and lean proteins, preventing blood sugar spikes. It supports daily vitality, mental clarity, and emotional balance without heavy or processed foods, complemented by an active lifestyle.

Prevention: Diabetes, Cholesterol, and Cancer
The Mediterranean Diet helps regulate blood sugar, improves cholesterol levels, and reduces inflammation, lowering the risk of diabetes, cardiovascular disease, and certain cancers. Antioxidant-rich foods and a balanced approach to eating support long-term health and disease prevention.

Chapter 3 – Nutritious and Easy Breakfasts

3.1 Black Olive and Tomato Whole Grain Focaccia

A hearty, flavorful flatbread infused with the earthiness of whole grains, the briny punch of black olives, and the vibrant sweetness of roasted cherry tomatoes.

BREAKFAST

Prep Time: 20 min / Servings x2

Black Olive and Tomato Whole Grain Focaccia

INGREDIENTS

- 2 cups whole wheat flour
- 1 cup all-purpose flour (or substitute with oat/barley flour for 100% whole grain)
- 1 tbsp active dry yeast
- 1 cup warm water (approx. 110°F / 45°C)
- 1 tsp sugar or honey
- 1 tsp sea salt
- 1/4 cup extra virgin olive oil (plus more for drizzling)
- 1/2 cup pitted black olives, sliced
- 1/2 cup cherry tomatoes, halved
- 1 tsp dried oregano or rosemary
- Coarse sea salt (for topping)

9

Preparation

1. Mix warm water, sugar/honey, and yeast. Let sit until frothy (5-10 minutes).
2. Combine flours and salt in a large bowl. Add the yeast mixture and 2 tbsp olive oil. Mix into a soft dough.
3. Knead for 5-7 minutes until smooth and elastic.
4. Place in an oiled bowl, cover, and let rise for about 1 hour or until doubled.
5. Press dough into a greased baking tray. Let rise another 20-30 minutes.
6. Dimple the dough with your fingers. Drizzle with oil. Press in olives and tomatoes. Sprinkle with herbs and salt. Bake at 425°F (220°C) for 20-25 minutes until golden.
7. Let rest slightly before slicing and serving.

Fat: ~8 g
Carbohydrates: ~25 g
Protein: ~5 g

The values are for 1 single dose

Scientific Background and Health Benefits

Whole wheat flour is rich in dietary fiber, magnesium, and B-vitamins, which contribute to digestive health, blood sugar regulation, and heart health. Tomatoes are a strong source of lycopene, a powerful antioxidant linked to reduced inflammation, skin protection, and potentially lower cancer risk. Black olives provide healthy monounsaturated fats, vitamin E, and natural polyphenols that support cardiovascular and cognitive function. The use of extra virgin olive oil aligns with the heart-healthy Mediterranean diet, known for its anti-inflammatory properties and benefits for longevity and metabolic balance.

Senior-Specific Notes

The soft, pillowy texture of focaccia makes it particularly suitable for older adults who may have difficulty chewing tougher breads. The combination of whole grains and healthy fats delivers sustained energy and essential nutrients, which are important for maintaining strength, mobility, and joint health. With low sugar and no saturated fats, this recipe supports heart health and is appropriate for those managing cholesterol or blood pressure. It's also easily customizable with flavor-rich, nutrient-dense toppings like onions, herbs, or roasted vegetables, without the need for excess salt or artificial ingredients.

Scan the QR to access the bonus: 7-day reset meal plan

3.2 Greek Yogurt with Honey and Walnuts

A creamy, protein-rich breakfast from Greece that combines natural sweetness with heart-healthy fats.

BREAKFAST

Greek Yogurt with Honey and Walnuts

Prep Time: 3 min / Servings x1

INGREDIENTS

- 1 cup (150g) plain Greek yogurt (preferably full-fat or 2%)
- 1 teaspoon natural honey
- 1 tablespoon chopped walnuts

Preparation

1. Spoon the Greek yogurt into a small bowl.
2. Drizzle the honey evenly over the top.
3. Sprinkle with chopped walnuts.
4. Enjoy immediately as a wholesome, creamy breakfast or a mid-morning snack.

Fat: ~12 g
Carbohydrates: ~18 g
Protein: ~10 g

The values are for 1 single dose

Scientific Background and Health Benefits

This traditional Greek breakfast offers a powerful combination of protein, healthy fats, and natural sugars.
Greek yogurt is high in protein and calcium, essential for maintaining muscle mass and strong bones in older adults. It also contains probiotics, which support gut health and immune function.
Walnuts are rich in omega-3 fatty acids, which contribute to heart and brain health. They also offer magnesium and antioxidants, helpful in reducing inflammation.

Honey, used in moderation, provides natural sweetness along with trace minerals and antimicrobial properties. It's also easier on blood sugar levels than refined sugars when paired with protein and fat, as in this recipe.
Studies show that regular consumption of fermented dairy products like Greek yogurt is linked to better digestive health, bone density, and even reduced risk of type 2 diabetes. Walnuts, meanwhile, have been associated with improved cognitive function and cardiovascular protection in seniors.

Senior-Specific Notes

- Soft and easy to chew—ideal for those with dental issues.
- High in calcium and protein to help prevent osteoporosis and muscle loss (sarcopenia).
- Probiotic-rich for better digestion and immune support.
- Can be adapted for diabetic diets by reducing or omitting the honey.
- A quick, no-prep option for independent living or caregivers looking for fast nutrition.

3.3 Bruschetta

An iconic Italian starter turned healthy senior-friendly snack: toasted whole grain bread topped with ripe tomatoes, fresh basil, and a drizzle of golden olive oil—a Mediterranean classic bursting with flavor and vitality.

BREAKFAST

Bruschetta

Prep Time: 15 min / Servings x2

INGREDIENTS

- 1 baguette or rustic whole grain loaf, sliced
- 2 cups ripe tomatoes, finely diced (cherry or Roma preferred)
- 2-3 cloves garlic (1 minced, 2 whole)
- 1/4 cup fresh basil leaves, chopped
- 2 tbsp extra virgin olive oil (plus more for drizzling)
- Salt and black pepper, to taste
- Optional: a splash of balsamic vinegar or glaze for serving

Preparation

1. In a bowl, combine diced tomatoes, minced garlic, chopped basil, olive oil, salt, and pepper. Let it sit for 10 minutes to marinate and enhance flavor.
2. Lightly brush bread slices with olive oil. Toast on a grill pan or in the oven at 400°F (200°C) for 5-7 minutes, or until golden and crisp.
3. While the bread is still warm, gently rub one side of each slice with a whole garlic clove for extra flavor.
4. Spoon the tomato mixture generously onto each toasted slice. Optionally drizzle with balsamic vinegar or glaze.
5. Best enjoyed fresh, while the bread is still crunchy and the tomatoes juicy.

Fat: ~7 g
Carbohydrates: ~22 g
Protein: ~4 g

The values are for 1 single dose

Scientific Background and Health Benefits

Bruschetta combines antioxidant-rich tomatoes with heart-protective olive oil and whole grain bread, creating a nutrient-dense appetizer with minimal processing. The tomatoes provide lycopene, vitamin C, and potassium, all of which support immune health and blood pressure regulation. Fresh basil contributes plant-based compounds with anti-inflammatory and antimicrobial effects, while garlic has been linked to cardiovascular benefits due to its ability to reduce blood pressure and cholesterol. Olive oil, the cornerstone of the Mediterranean diet, offers healthy fats that enhance nutrient absorption and support long-term heart and brain health.

Senior-Specific Notes

Bruschetta is an excellent choice for seniors thanks to its light, digestible ingredients and its balance of flavor without heaviness. The tomatoes and basil are hydrating and rich in vitamins, which is helpful in supporting immunity and skin health. If chewing crisp bread is a concern, the toast can be made slightly softer or served with the topping on the side. The garlic and olive oil also support heart health and circulation, making this a smart and flavorful addition to a senior-friendly menu.

3.4 Fresh Seasonal Fruit

A vibrant, refreshing assortment of ripe, in-season fruits, served raw and at their peak of flavor and nutritional value.

20

BREAKFAST

Fresh Seasonal Fruit

Prep Time: 10 min / Servings x2

INGREDIENTS

Spring
- Strawberries
- Pineapple
- Kiwi
- Blood oranges
- Fresh mint

Summer
- Watermelon
- Cherries
- Blueberries
- Mango
- Peaches
- Basil or lime zest for garnish

Autumn
- Apples
- Pears
- Grapes
- Persimmons
- Pomegranate seeds
- Cinnamon sprinkle (optional)

Winter
- Citrus fruits (oranges, grapefruit, mandarins)
- Kiwi
- Bananas
- Dried figs or dates (optional for texture contrast)

Preparation

1. Wash and dry all fruit thoroughly.
2. Slice or dice into bite-sized pieces, depending on the type and presentation.
3. Arrange attractively in a shallow bowl, platter, or layered parfait-style.
4. Garnish with fresh herbs like mint or basil, or a sprinkle of lemon/lime juice for extra brightness.
5. Serve immediately to preserve freshness and prevent browning.

Fat: ~1 g
Carbohydrates: ~20 g
Protein: ~1 g

The values are for 1 single dose

Scientific Background and Health Benefits

Fresh fruit is naturally rich in vitamins, minerals, fiber, and antioxidants. Seasonal fruit, in particular, tends to have higher nutrient density due to being harvested at peak ripeness. Common benefits include immune support from vitamin C (citrus, berries), digestive regulation from fiber (apples, pears), and heart health support from potassium and polyphenols (bananas, grapes, pomegranate). Unlike fruit juices, whole fruit contains fiber that helps regulate blood sugar and promotes satiety.

Senior-Specific Notes

Fresh seasonal fruit is ideal for older adults, offering hydration, gentle sweetness, and easily digestible nutrients. Soft fruits like berries, melon, and citrus segments are especially easy to chew and swallow. The high antioxidant content helps fight cellular aging, while fiber supports gut health and cholesterol management. For those with blood sugar concerns, pairing fruit with a source of healthy fat (like nuts or yogurt) can help reduce glycemic impact.

3.5 Gluten-Free Fig Olive Oil Cake

A beautifully moist and subtly sweet cake that captures the essence of the Mediterranean through ripe figs and silky extra virgin olive oil.

BREAKFAST

Prep Time: 40 min / Servings x2

Gluten-Free Fig Olive Oil Cake

INGREDIENTS

- 1 ½ cups almond flour
- ¼ cup coconut flour
- 1 tsp baking soda
- ¼ tsp salt
- 3 large eggs
- ⅓ cup extra virgin olive oil
- ⅓ cup raw honey or maple syrup
- 1 tsp vanilla extract
- 1 tsp apple cider vinegar
- 6-8 fresh figs, sliced (or use dried figs, chopped, if not in season)
- Optional: ½ tsp ground cinnamon or lemon zest for added flavor

Preparation

1. Preheat your oven to 350°F (175°C). Line an 8-inch round cake pan with parchment paper or lightly grease it.
2. Mix the dry ingredients: In a medium bowl, whisk together almond flour, coconut flour, baking soda, salt, and cinnamon (if using).
3. Mix the wet ingredients: In a separate large bowl, beat the eggs, then whisk in olive oil, honey or maple syrup, vanilla, and apple cider vinegar.
4. Combine the dry mixture with the wet, stirring just until smooth. The batter will be thick.
5. Pour the batter into the prepared pan and smooth the top. Arrange fig slices on top in a decorative pattern, gently pressing them into the surface.
6. Bake for 35–40 minutes, or until golden brown and a toothpick inserted in the center comes out clean.
7. Cool in the pan for 10 minutes, then transfer to a wire rack to cool completely.
8. Serve as-is or with a drizzle of honey, a dusting of almond meal, or a dollop of whipped coconut cream.

Fat: ~14 g
Carbohydrates: ~30 g
Protein: ~3 g

The values are for 1 single dose

Scientific Background and Health Benefits

This cake is a wholesome alternative to traditional desserts, made entirely without grains, dairy, or refined sugar. Almond flour provides plant-based protein, fiber, and vitamin E, supporting satiety and skin health. Olive oil is rich in heart-healthy monounsaturated fats and antioxidants. Figs add natural sweetness along with fiber, calcium, and potassium, supporting digestion and bone health. The honey or maple syrup keeps the glycemic load lower compared to processed sugars, making this a gentler option for blood sugar regulation.

Senior-Specific Notes

Soft and moist in texture, this cake is easy to chew and digest, making it ideal for older adults. The healthy fats and natural fibers support energy levels, cognitive function, and cardiovascular health. Figs contribute gentle sweetness and important minerals like calcium and magnesium, which are vital for aging bones and muscle function. Because it's lower in sugar and made without gluten, it's a safer indulgence for those managing blood sugar, inflammation, or dietary sensitivities.

Chapter 4 – Balanced Lunches for Energy and Digestion

4.1 Legume and Spelt Soup

A traditional Italian soup that combines hearty legumes and ancient grains for lasting energy and gentle digestion.

LUNCH

Prep Time: 45 min / Servings x2

Legume and Spelt Soup

INGREDIENTS

- ½ cup dried mixed legumes (or 1½ cups cooked/canned, rinsed) – e.g., lentils, chickpeas, cannellini beans
- ¼ cup spelt (soaked overnight or quick-cooking variety)
- 1 carrot, chopped
- 1 celery stalk, chopped
- ½ onion, finely chopped
- 2 tablespoons extra virgin olive oil
- 1 clove garlic, minced
- 1 sprig of rosemary or 1 bay leaf
- 1 liter (4 cups) of water or low-sodium vegetable broth
- Salt and black pepper to taste

29

Preparation

1. If using dried legumes and whole spelt, soak them overnight, then drain and rinse.
2. In a large pot, heat the olive oil and sauté the onion, garlic, carrot, and celery for about 5 minutes until softened.
3. Add the legumes, spelt, herbs, and broth or water. Bring to a boil, then reduce the heat and let it simmer for 45–60 minutes, or until everything is tender.
4. Remove the herbs and season with salt and pepper. If desired, blend a portion of the soup for a creamier texture.
5. Serve hot, drizzled with a little extra virgin olive oil and a slice of whole grain bread on the side.

Fat: ~5 g
Carbohydrates: ~30 g
Protein: ~10 g

The values are for 1 single dose

Scientific Background and Health Benefits

This soup is a nutritional powerhouse, combining protein, fiber, and slow-releasing carbohydrates—all essential for sustained energy and digestive support.

Legumes (beans, lentils, chickpeas) are rich in plant-based protein, fiber, iron, and folate. They help lower cholesterol, stabilize blood sugar, and support heart health.

Spelt, one of the oldest grains in the Mediterranean tradition, is high in fiber and minerals like magnesium and iron, which aid muscle function and combat fatigue.

The vegetables provide antioxidants, vitamins, and hydration, while olive oil adds healthy fats that improve nutrient absorption and reduce inflammation.

Studies show that regular consumption of legumes and whole grains is associated with reduced risk of heart disease, type 2 diabetes, and colorectal cancer—conditions that commonly affect aging adults.

Senior-Specific Notes

- Easy to digest and full of fiber—supports healthy bowel movements and gut health.
- Can be blended for those with chewing or swallowing difficulties.
- High in plant-based protein, perfect for seniors eating less meat.
- Provides long-lasting energy without spikes in blood sugar.
- Freezable and easy to batch-cook for convenience or caregivers.

4.2 Ensalada de Garbanzos

A refreshing Spanish chickpea salad full of flavor, fiber, and heart-healthy ingredients—perfect for a light, energizing lunch.

32

LUNCH

Prep Time: 10 min / Servings x2

Ensalada de Garbanzos

INGREDIENTS

- 1½ cups cooked or canned chickpeas (rinsed and drained)
- ½ red bell pepper, diced
- ½ cucumber, diced
- ½ small red onion, thinly sliced
- 1 small tomato, chopped
- 2 tablespoons extra virgin olive oil
- Juice of ½ lemon
- 1 tablespoon chopped fresh parsley
- Salt and black pepper to taste
- Optional: a few black olives or a pinch of ground cumin for added flavor

Preparation

1. In a large bowl, combine the chickpeas, bell pepper, cucumber, onion, and tomato.
2. In a small bowl, whisk together the olive oil and lemon juice.
3. Pour the dressing over the salad, mix well, and season with salt and pepper.
4. Add chopped parsley and optional olives or spices.
5. Let the salad rest for 10 minutes before serving to enhance the flavors. Serve chilled or at room temperature.

Fat: ~10 g
Carbohydrates: ~20 g
Protein: ~8 g

The values are for 1 single dose

Scientific Background and Health Benefits

Chickpeas are one of the most valuable legumes in the Mediterranean diet. They are rich in plant-based protein, fiber, iron, and magnesium, helping to maintain muscle mass, support digestive health, and regulate blood sugar.
 Vegetables like cucumber, bell pepper, and tomato provide hydration, vitamin C, potassium, and antioxidants that support heart and immune health.
Olive oil and lemon juice add anti-inflammatory properties and help the body absorb fat-soluble vitamins like A, D, and E.
Multiple studies have linked legume-based meals with lower cholesterol, improved glycemic control, and reduced inflammation—all critical factors in chronic disease prevention for seniors.

Senior-Specific Notes

- Requires no cooking—ideal for hot days or low-energy mealtimes.
- Soft texture, easy to chew and swallow.
- High in fiber and protein, which helps with satiety and blood sugar stability.
- Light yet nutrient-dense—great for smaller appetites.
- Can be prepared in advance and stored for 1–2 days in the fridge.

4.3 Mediterranean Salad Grilled Octopus

A vibrant and refreshing dish that combines tender grilled octopus with a classic Greek-style salad of tomatoes, cucumber, olives, and herbs.

36

LUNCH

Prep Time: 55 min / Servings x2

Ensalada de Garbanzos

INGREDIENTS

- For the octopus:
- 1 whole octopus (600-800 g / 1.3-1.7 lbs), fresh or thawed
- 1 bay leaf
- ½ lemon
- 1 tbsp white wine vinegar

- For the salad:
- 1 cucumber
- 2 ripe tomatoes
- ½ red onion (sweet variety)
- Kalamata olives, to taste
- 1 tbsp capers, rinsed

37

Preparation

1. Cook the octopus:
   - In a large pot, bring water to a boil with bay leaf, lemon, and vinegar.
   - Dip the octopus 2-3 times to curl the tentacles, then let it simmer gently for 40-50 minutes.
   - Let it cool in its own broth for extra flavor and tenderness.
2. Grill the octopus:
   - Slice the tentacles and grill them on a hot grill or skillet for a few minutes until slightly crispy and charred.
   - Brush lightly with olive oil and add a pinch of pepper.
3. Make the salad:
   - Dice the tomatoes and cucumber. Thinly slice the red onion.
   - Combine all salad ingredients in a bowl: veggies, olives, capers, and feta if using.
   - Season with olive oil, lemon juice, oregano, and mix gently.
4. Serve:
   - Plate the salad and top with warm grilled octopus.
   - Drizzle with extra olive oil and sprinkle fresh parsley if desired.

Fat: ~9 g
Carbohydrates: ~6 g
Protein: ~20 g

The values are for 1 single dose

Senior-Friendly Tips

Lean protein, Octopus is high in digestible protein and low in fat. Heart-healthy fats, because olive oil, olives, and optional feta offer monounsaturated fats.
 Digestive support, because lemon juice enhances iron absorption and digestion.
 Low-sodium option. Reduce or omit capers and feta for those with high blood pressure.

4.4 Mediterranean-Style Shrimps

A fresh and flavorful dish featuring tender shrimp sautéed with cherry tomatoes, garlic, fresh parsley, and extra virgin olive oil – finished with a splash of lemon.

LUNCH

Prep Time: 10 min / Servings x2

Mediterranean-Style Shrimps

INGREDIENTS

- 300g (about 10 oz) peeled and deveined shrimp
- 2 tbsp extra virgin olive oil
- 1 garlic clove
- 10-12 cherry tomatoes, halved
- Juice of ½ lemon
- Fresh parsley, chopped (to taste)
- Salt and black pepper (to taste)
- Optional: a pinch of chili flakes for heat

Preparation

1. Heat the olive oil in a non-stick skillet over medium heat. Add the whole garlic clove and sauté for 1-2 minutes until fragrant, then remove it.
2. Add the cherry tomatoes, cooking for 3-4 minutes until they begin to soften and release their juices.
3. Add the shrimp, season with salt, pepper, and chili flakes if using. Sauté for 4-5 minutes, turning once, until the shrimp are pink and fully cooked.
4. Finish with lemon juice and chopped parsley, tossing gently to coat.
5. Serve warm, on its own or with a side of whole grain bread or fresh salad.

Fat: ~7 g
Carbohydrates: ~5 g
Protein: ~22 g

The values are for 1 single dose

Scientific Background and Health Benefits

This dish exemplifies the Mediterranean diet, known for promoting heart and metabolic health. Shrimp provide lean protein, vitamin B12, and key minerals like selenium and iodine. Extra virgin olive oil contains monounsaturated fats and polyphenols that combat inflammation and support brain and cardiovascular function. Tomatoes are rich in lycopene and vitamin C, offering antioxidant protection. Combined, these ingredients support muscle health, immunity, and a balanced glycemic response.

Senior-Specific Notes

Mediterranean-style shrimp is an ideal choice for older adults. It's soft in texture and easy to chew, high in protein to support muscle mass, and naturally low in saturated fats. The dish is light on the digestive system and provides anti-inflammatory nutrients that may help manage conditions like arthritis and high cholesterol. The citrus and herbs add brightness without the need for heavy seasoning or sauces, making it suitable even for reduced salt diets.

Scan the QR to access the bonus: Greek Sweets

4.5 Pisto Manchego with Egg

A traditional Spanish vegetable medley topped with a softly cooked egg—simple, nourishing, and full of Mediterranean flavor.

44

LUNCH

Prep Time: 35 min / Servings x2

Pisto Manchego with Egg

INGREDIENTS

- 1 small zucchini, diced
- 1 small eggplant, diced
- 1 red bell pepper, diced
- 1 small onion, chopped
- 1 garlic clove, minced
- 2 ripe tomatoes, chopped (or 1 cup canned peeled tomatoes)
- 2 tablespoons extra virgin olive oil
- 2 eggs
- Salt and pepper to taste
- Optional: a pinch of smoked paprika or chopped parsley for garnish

Preparation

1. Heat olive oil in a large skillet over medium heat. Add the chopped onion and garlic and sauté for 3-4 minutes until softened.
2. Add the bell pepper, zucchini, and eggplant. Stir and cook for about 10 minutes, until the vegetables begin to soften.
3. Add the chopped tomatoes, salt, pepper, and optional paprika. Reduce heat, cover, and simmer for 20-25 minutes until all vegetables are tender and the sauce is thick.
4. Make two small wells in the vegetable mixture. Crack one egg into each well. Cover the pan again and cook for 5-7 minutes, or until the eggs are just set.
5. Serve hot, optionally garnished with fresh parsley and a slice of whole grain bread.

Fat: ~14 g
Carbohydrates: ~12 g
Protein: ~8 g

The values are for 1 single dose

Scientific Background and Health Benefits

TThis classic dish from La Mancha, Spain, is a plant-based meal rich in fiber, antioxidants, and heart-protective nutrients.

Eggplant, zucchini, and peppers offer a wide range of vitamins (A, C, and K), as well as potassium and hydration.

Tomatoes provide lycopene, a powerful antioxidant linked to reduced inflammation and improved cardiovascular health.

Eggs are a complete protein source, rich in B vitamins, choline, and selenium, all of which support cognitive function and cellular repair.

Olive oil, a key Mediterranean ingredient, enhances nutrient absorption and protects against heart disease and oxidative stress.

Pisto's nutritional profile makes it ideal for maintaining energy levels, gut health, and cognitive clarity—especially important for older adults.

Senior-Specific Notes

- The soft texture is easy to chew and digest.
- Eggs add a satisfying protein boost without heaviness.
- Can be served warm or at room temperature—gentle on digestion.
- Excellent choice for seniors with reduced appetite or chewing difficulties.
- Can be made ahead and reheated; ideal for caregivers or batch cooking.

Scan the QR to access the bonus: 4-week meal plan

Chapter 5 – Light but Flavorful Dinners

5.1 Psari Plaki (Baked Fish with Tomato)

A classic Greek dish where white fish is gently baked in a fragrant tomato and herb sauce—light, heart-healthy, and full of Mediterranean warmth.

DINNER

Psari Plaki (Baked Fish with Tomato)

Prep Time: 30 min / Servings x2

INGREDIENTS

- 2 white fish fillets (e.g., cod, hake, or sea bass)
- 2 ripe tomatoes, chopped (or 1 cup canned peeled tomatoes)
- ½ onion, thinly sliced
- 1 garlic clove, minced
- 2 tablespoons extra virgin olive oil
- Juice of ½ lemon
- 1 tablespoon chopped fresh parsley
- ½ teaspoon dried oregano
- Salt and pepper to taste
- Optional: a few slices of zucchini or bell pepper for added vegetables

Preparation

1. Preheat the oven to 180°C (350°F).
2. In a pan, heat 1 tablespoon of olive oil and gently sauté the onion and garlic until soft. Add the chopped tomatoes, oregano, salt, and pepper, and simmer for about 10 minutes until the sauce thickens slightly.
3. Place the fish fillets in a lightly oiled baking dish. Pour the tomato sauce over the top.
4. Add lemon juice and a drizzle of the remaining olive oil.
5. Cover the dish with foil and bake for 20–25 minutes, until the fish is cooked through and flakes easily with a fork.
6. Garnish with chopped parsley and serve warm, optionally with steamed vegetables or a small portion of whole grain rice.

Fat: ~10 g
Carbohydrates: ~8 g
Protein: ~23 g

The values are for 1 single dose

Scientific Background and Health Benefits

TPsari Plaki is a shining example of the Mediterranean way of eating—light, clean, and packed with protective nutrients.

White fish is an excellent source of lean protein and is rich in vitamin B12, iodine, and selenium, all essential for metabolic health and brain function.

Tomatoes and olive oil are a perfect pairing—tomatoes provide lycopene (a powerful antioxidant), and olive oil enhances its absorption while also reducing inflammation.

Lemon juice adds vitamin C and supports digestion, while herbs like oregano and parsley contribute anti-inflammatory and antimicrobial properties.

Studies have consistently shown that increasing fish intake—especially when paired with antioxidant-rich vegetables—supports cardiovascular health, helps maintain cognitive function, and may reduce the risk of chronic diseases common in later life.

Senior-Specific Notes

- Very easy to chew and digest—ideal for those with dental or swallowing issues.
- Light, non-greasy, and hydrating—perfect for evening meals.
- High in protein and healthy fats, which support muscle maintenance and brain health.
- Can be cooked in batches and gently reheated without losing flavor or texture.
- Gentle on the stomach and suitable for those with reduced appetite or sensitive digestion.

5.2 Moussaka

Moussaka is a layered oven-baked casserole, most famously part of Greek cuisine.

DINNER

Moussaka

Prep Time: 45 min / Servings x2

INGREDIENTS

- For the vegetable base:
- 2-3 large eggplants, sliced lengthwise
- Olive oil, for brushing
- Salt

For the meat sauce:
- 500g ground lamb or beef
- 1 onion, finely chopped
- 2 cloves garlic, minced
- 400g canned crushed tomatoes
- 2 tbsp tomato paste
- 1/2 tsp cinnamon
- 1/4 tsp ground allspice or nutmeg
- Salt and black pepper, to taste
- Optional: a splash of red wine

For the béchamel topping:

- 4 tbsp butter (or olive oil for dairy-free)
- 4 tbsp flour (or gluten-free alternative)
- 2 cups milk (or plant-based milk)
- 1 egg yolk
- Pinch of nutmeg
- Salt and pepper
- Optional: grated cheese (kefalotyri, Parmesan, or dairy-free option)

Preparation

1. Salt the slices and let them sit for 30 minutes to remove bitterness. Pat dry, brush with olive oil, and roast at 400°F (200°C) for 20-25 minutes, flipping once.
2. MSauté onions and garlic in olive oil. Add the ground meat and cook until browned. Stir in tomato paste, crushed tomatoes, spices, and wine if using. Simmer for 20-30 minutes until thickened.
3. Make the béchamel:
4. In a saucepan, melt butter, stir in flour to make a roux, then slowly whisk in milk until smooth. Cook until thick, then remove from heat and stir in egg yolk, nutmeg, and cheese if using.
5. In a baking dish, layer eggplant slices, then meat sauce, repeating once or twice. Finish with the béchamel spread evenly over the top.
6. Bake at 375°F (190°C) for 45-60 minutes, until golden and bubbling. Let cool slightly before slicing to help it set.

Fat: ~18 g
Carbohydrates: ~15 g
Protein: ~12 g

The values are for 1 single dose

Scientific Background and Health Benefits

Eggplants are high in antioxidants (like nasunin), fiber, and polyphenols that support heart and brain health. The olive oil and tomato-based meat sauce provide monounsaturated fats and lycopene, which are beneficial for inflammation and cholesterol. While béchamel adds richness, making it with plant milk or olive oil lightens the dish. Using lamb provides iron and zinc, while a beef version is typically leaner.

Senior-Specific Notes

Moussaka can be made softer by thinly slicing the eggplants and cooking them thoroughly, making it easy to chew. It offers protein, fiber, and healthy fats – important for muscle maintenance and cardiovascular health in older adults. The warming spices are gentle and aromatic, helping digestion and appetite. For a lighter option, the béchamel can be made dairy-free or with less fat, while still retaining its satisfying character.

Scan the QR to access the bonus: 7-day reset meal plan

5.3 Lemon Sardines

A light, zesty dish featuring fresh sardines marinated or grilled with lemon juice, garlic, olive oil, and herbs.

DINNER

Lemon Sardines

Prep Time: 15 min / Servings x2

INGREDIENTS

- 500g (about 1 lb) fresh sardines, cleaned and gutted
- 2 tbsp extra virgin olive oil
- 2 cloves garlic, finely sliced
- Juice of 1 lemon
- Zest of ½ lemon
- Fresh parsley, chopped (to taste)
- Salt and black pepper, to taste
- Breadcrumbs (100g)
- Optional: a pinch of chili flakes or dried oregano

Preparation

1. Prepare the sardines: Open them like a book (if they aren't already) and place them on paper towels to let them dry a bit.
2. Make the breadcrumb mixture: In a bowl, mix together breadcrumbs, minced garlic, chopped parsley, a pinch of salt, pepper, and (if you like) a handful of grated Parmesan. Add a drizzle of olive oil and stir until the mixture is moist, not dry.
3. Arrange the sardines: Place them on a baking tray lined with parchment paper, skin side down. Top each sardine with a spoonful of the breadcrumb mixture, pressing it down gently.
4. Bake: Cook in a preheated oven at 200°C (390°F) for about 10-12 minutes, or until the topping is golden and crispy.
5. Serve: Finish with a squeeze of lemon and maybe a fresh side salad.

Fat: ~12 g
Carbohydrates: ~1 g
Protein: ~20 g

The values are for 1 single dose

Scientific Background and Health Benefits

ESardines are a powerhouse of nutrients – rich in omega-3 fatty acids, calcium (especially if consumed with bones), vitamin D, and high-quality protein. Regular consumption supports heart health, brain function, and bone strength. Lemon adds vitamin C and enhances iron absorption from the fish. Olive oil contributes monounsaturated fats and antioxidants that fight inflammation and support cardiovascular wellness.

Senior-Specific Notes

Sardines are excellent for older adults thanks to their soft texture, small size, and nutrient density. They're especially valuable for maintaining bone density (calcium and vitamin D), supporting memory (omega-3s), and heart function. The preparation is gentle on digestion, and the citrus makes the dish flavorful without requiring excess salt or sauces. For even easier consumption, the fish can be deboned and served flaked over soft vegetables or whole grain toast.

5.4 Cuttlefish and Peas

A traditional Italian coastal dish combining tender cuttlefish (seppie) and sweet green peas, simmered together in a delicate tomato-based sauce or in bianco (without tomato).

60

DINNER
Cuttlefish and Peas

Prep Time: 45 min / Servings x2

INGREDIENTS

- 800g (about 1.75 lb) cuttlefish (cleaned and cut into strips or bite-sized pieces)
- 300g (about 10 oz) green peas (fresh or frozen)
- 1 small onion, finely chopped
- 2-3 tbsp extra virgin olive oil
- 1/2 glass dry white wine
- 200g (about 7 oz) tomato passata (optional – for the red version)
- Salt and pepper to taste
- Fresh parsley for garnish
- Optional: a pinch of chili flakes or a bay leaf for aromatic depth

Preparation

1. Sauté the onion in olive oil over medium heat until soft and translucent.
2. Add the cuttlefish, cook for a few minutes until it begins to release its juices. Pour in the white wine and let it evaporate.
3. (Optional) Add the tomato passata and stir to coat. If preparing in bianco, skip the tomato and just add a bit of water or broth.
4. Simmer gently for about 20-25 minutes, covering the pot halfway.
5. Add the peas, season with salt and pepper, and continue cooking for another 15-20 minutes until the peas are tender and the seppie are soft.
6. Finish with fresh parsley, and serve hot, optionally accompanied by soft polenta or crusty bread.

Fat: ~8 g
Carbohydrates: ~9 g
Protein: ~20 g

The values are for 1 single dose

Scientific Background and Health Benefits

Cuttlefish is a low-fat, high-protein seafood rich in selenium, B vitamins, and phosphorus, supporting muscle health and metabolic function. Peas add plant-based fiber, protein, and micronutrients like vitamin K and folate. Cooked in extra virgin olive oil and optionally enhanced with tomato (rich in lycopene), this dish aligns perfectly with the principles of the Mediterranean diet, offering anti-inflammatory benefits, heart support, and digestive ease.

Senior-Specific Notes

Seppie con piselli is soft in texture and easy to chew, making it ideal for older adults. It provides lean, digestible protein and essential nutrients for maintaining bone density, immune function, and energy. The use of olive oil and mild seasoning supports heart health and reduces strain on the digestive system. For even easier digestion, finely chopping the seppie and lightly mashing the peas can create a smoother consistency.

5.5 Baked Sea Bream with Fennel and Lemon

A delicate and aromatic Italian dish featuring oven-baked sea bream infused with fennel and lemon—light, flavorful, and rich in heart-healthy nutrients.

DINNER

Baked Sea Bream with Fennel and Lemon

Prep Time: 30 min / Servings x2

INGREDIENTS

- 2 small sea breams (or fillets), cleaned
- 1 small fennel bulb, thinly sliced
- 1 lemon, sliced
- 1 tablespoon extra-virgin olive oil
- 1 garlic clove, minced
- A few sprigs of fresh parsley or thyme
- Salt and black pepper to taste
- Optional: splash of white wine (for steaming)

Preparation

1. Preheat the oven to 180°C (350°F).
2. In a baking dish, layer the sliced fennel and a few lemon slices to create a bed for the fish.
3. Place the sea bream on top (whole or fillets). Sprinkle with salt, pepper, garlic, and herbs.
4. Top with additional lemon slices and drizzle everything with olive oil. Add a splash of white wine if desired.
5. Cover with foil and bake for 20–25 minutes, or until the fish is flaky and cooked through.
6. Serve warm with a side of lightly steamed vegetables or a small portion of boiled potatoes.

Fat: ~9 g
Carbohydrates: ~4 g
Protein: ~24 g

The values are for 1 single dose

Scientific Background and Health Benefits

This dish highlights the Mediterranean balance of lean protein, aromatic vegetables, and healthy fats.
Sea bream is a light, flaky fish rich in high-quality protein, omega-3 fatty acids, and essential minerals like selenium, iodine, and vitamin D, all of which support brain, thyroid, and cardiovascular health.
Fennel aids digestion, reduces bloating, and provides fiber, vitamin C, and potassium.
Lemon adds a boost of antioxidants and supports digestion and immune function, while olive oil enhances heart protection and nutrient absorption.
Fish-based dinners are linked to improved heart rhythm, reduced inflammation, and better cognitive performance—especially important for seniors.

Senior-Specific Notes

- Very soft and easy to chew—ideal for sensitive teeth or digestion.
- Naturally low in sodium—great for managing blood pressure.
- Light and non-bloating—perfect for evening meals.
- The gentle flavor is pleasing to mild palates, and fennel supports digestive comfort.
- Easily digestible and can be scaled for solo or shared meals.

.

Chapter 6 – Healthy Snacks Throughout the Day

6.1 Black Olive Tapenade with Crostini

A savory Spanish-inspired spread made from black olives, perfect on crispy crostini for a flavorful and healthy Mediterranean snack.
.

SNACKS

Prep Time: 10 min / Servings x2

Black Olive Tapenade with Crostini

INGREDIENTS

- For the tapenade:
- 1 cup pitted black olives (preferably Spanish or Kalamata)
- 1 tablespoon capers (rinsed)
- 1 clove garlic (optional, for a stronger flavor)
- 2 tablespoons extra virgin olive oil
- 1 teaspoon lemon juice or red wine vinegar
- Optional: a few fresh parsleys leaves or thyme
- For the crostini:
- 4-6 slices of whole grain or sourdough baguette
- A drizzle of olive oil

69

Preparation

1. Preheat the oven to 180°C (350°F). Lightly brush the bread slices with olive oil and toast in the oven for 5-7 minutes, until golden and crisp.
2. In a food processor or with a hand blender, blend the olives, capers, lemon juice, and herbs with olive oil until you get a coarse paste. Adjust texture to your liking.
3. Spread a small amount of tapenade on each crostino. Serve immediately, or store the tapenade in the fridge for up to 3 days.

Fat: ~11 g
Carbohydrates: ~14 g
Protein: ~3 g

The values are for 1 single dose

Scientific Background and Health Benefits

This savory snack is full of monounsaturated fats, antioxidants, and flavor compounds that promote cardiovascular health without relying on sugars or refined carbs.

Black olives are a source of healthy fats, vitamin E, and polyphenols, which help reduce inflammation and support blood vessel function.

Capers and olive oil offer additional antioxidant protection and enhance digestion.

Compared to typical snacks, this option is lower in calories, more filling, and packed with healthy fats—making it perfect for heart and brain support.

Studies have shown that diets rich in olives and olive oil contribute to lower cholesterol, better blood pressure regulation, and slower cognitive decline, particularly in older adults.

Senior-Specific Notes

- Easy to spread and chew—especially when served on soft or lightly toasted bread.
- Can be served on veggie sticks (like cucumber or bell pepper) for a low-carb, tooth-friendly option.
- Full of flavor, which helps stimulate appetite in seniors with reduced taste perception.
- A healthy alternative to processed snacks like crackers or chips.
- Can be made in advance and used for several snacks or light meals.

6.2 Feta with Cucumber and Oregano

A light and cooling Greek snack made with creamy feta, crisp cucumber, and a sprinkle of oregano—simple, hydrating, and full of flavor.

72

SNACKS

Feta with Cucumber and Oregano

Prep Time: 5 min / Servings x2

INGREDIENTS

- 50–60g (about 2 oz) feta cheese, cut into cubes or slices
- ½ cucumber, peeled and sliced into rounds or sticks
- 1 tablespoon extra-virgin olive oil
- A pinch of dried oregano
- Optional: a few drops of lemon juice or freshly ground black pepper

Preparation

1. Arrange the cucumber slices or sticks on a small plate.
2. Add cubes or slices of feta cheese on top or on the side.
3. Drizzle with olive oil and sprinkle with dried oregano.
4. Add lemon juice or pepper if desired. Serve immediately as a quick, satisfying snack or light appetizer.

Fat: ~10 g
Carbohydrates: ~3 g
Protein: ~6 g

The values are for 1 single dose

Scientific Background and Health Benefits

This snack balances hydration, protein, and flavor—a perfect example of the Mediterranean approach to healthy snacking.
Cucumber is over 90% water, making it ideal for hydration, especially for seniors who may forget to drink fluids. It also provides potassium, which helps regulate blood pressure.
Feta cheese is rich in calcium, protein, and probiotics (if traditionally made), all of which support bone health, digestion, and muscle maintenance.
Oregano adds antioxidant and antimicrobial benefits, while olive oil brings heart-protective monounsaturated fats.
This combination delivers nourishment and flavor without heaviness or refined carbs—ideal for maintaining energy and satiety between meals.

Senior-Specific Notes

- Very easy to chew—soft cheese and raw cucumber require minimal effort.
- High in calcium and protein—supports bones and muscles.
- Naturally low in carbs and sugar—good for blood sugar control.
- Quick and satisfying for small appetites or mid-afternoon hunger.
- Can be served chilled, making it especially refreshing in warm weather.

6.3 Mixed Dried Fruit

A naturally sweet and portable Italian snack rich in fiber, minerals, and tradition—ideal for a gentle energy boost anytime.

76

SNACKS
Mixed Dried Fruit

Prep Time: none / Servings x1

INGREDIENTS

- A small handful (approx. 30g) of mixed dried fruits such as:
- Dried figs
- Dried apricots
- Raisins or sultanas
- Dried prunes
- Dried apples or pears
- Optional: 2-3 whole almonds or walnuts (for added texture and healthy fats)

Preparation

1. Portion a small handful of your favorite dried fruits into a bowl or snack container.
2. Add a few nuts if desired for extra crunch and nutrition.
3. Enjoy as a mid-morning or mid-afternoon snack, or serve alongside an herbal tea.

Fat: ~3 g
Carbohydrates: ~25 g
Protein: ~2 g

The values are for 1 single dose

Scientific Background and Health Benefits

In Italian culture, dried fruits have long been enjoyed for their natural sweetness, long shelf life, and digestive benefits.
Dried figs, apricots, and prunes are rich in dietary fiber, which supports bowel regularity and helps control cholesterol.
They also provide essential minerals like potassium, magnesium, and iron, which are important for heart health, nerve function, and preventing anemia in older adults.
A small serving offers a gentle energy lift from natural sugars, without the blood sugar spike that comes from processed snacks.
Prunes, in particular, have been shown to improve bone health and reduce inflammation—making them especially valuable in a senior's diet.

Senior-Specific Notes

- Naturally soft and chewy—easy on the teeth and gums.
- Excellent for supporting digestive regularity and gut health.
- Convenient and portable—ideal for independent seniors or caregivers.
- Should be portioned mindfully due to concentrated sugars.
- Can be soaked in warm water for a few minutes if extra softness is needed.

Scan the QR to access the bonus: Greek Sweets

6.4 Fresh Fruit with Lemon Zest

A light and refreshing Italian snack or dessert that combines seasonal fruit with a touch of citrus—simple, elegant, and naturally energizing.

80

SNACKS

Fresh Fruit with Lemon Zest

Prep Time: 5 / Servings x1

INGREDIENTS

- 1 cup fresh seasonal fruit, cut into bite-sized pieces (e.g. apple, pear, peach, orange, grapes, melon, or berries)
- Zest of ½ organic lemon
- Optional: a few mint leaves or a splash of lemon juice

Preparation

1. Wash and cut the fruit into small, easy-to-eat pieces. Choose ripe, in-season fruit for the best flavor and nutrition.
2. Arrange in a small bowl.
3. Using a fine grater or zester, sprinkle fresh lemon zest over the top.
4. Add mint or a squeeze of lemon juice for extra brightness, if desired.
5. Serve immediately as a refreshing snack, light dessert, or side with breakfast.

Fat: ~1 g
Carbohydrates: ~18 g
Protein: ~1 g

The values are for 1 single dose

Scientific Background and Health Benefits

This snack showcases the fresh, clean flavors of the Mediterranean diet while providing key nutrients that support senior health.

Fresh fruit is rich in fiber, vitamins, and antioxidants, including vitamin C, which supports immune function, skin health, and iron absorption.

Lemon zest adds an extra boost of antioxidants (especially flavonoids) and enzymes that may support digestion and help the body detoxify naturally.

Eating fruit with its natural fiber slows sugar absorption and supports gut health—especially helpful for seniors managing blood sugar levels or digestion.

Senior-Specific Notes

- Soft and easy to chew—ideal for those with sensitive teeth or chewing difficulties.
- Very hydrating—great for seniors who tend to drink too little.
- Can be customized to preferences or chewing ability (e.g., use melon or banana for extra softness).
- Light but nutrient-rich—perfect for smaller appetites.
- Stimulates the senses with natural sweetness and citrus aroma, which may boost appetite and mood.

Scan the QR to access the bonus: 4-week meal plan

6.5 Herbal Tea with Spelt and Sesame Cookies

A soothing Greek-inspired snack pairing mild herbal tea with fiber-rich, gently sweet cookies—perfect for a calm afternoon break.

84

SNACKS

Herbal Tea with Spelt and Sesame Cookies

Prep Time: 15 / Servings x2

INGREDIENTS

- For the herbal tea:
- 2 cups water
- 1 tablespoon dried Greek mountain tea, chamomile, or mint
- Optional: a slice of lemon or a drizzle of honey
- For the cookies (makes ~8 small):
- ¾ cup spelt flour
- 2 tablespoons sesame seeds
- 1 tablespoon olive oil
- 1 tablespoon honey or maple syrup
- ¼ teaspoon cinnamon
- 2-3 tablespoons water (as needed)

85

Preparation

1. For the tea:
2. Bring the water to a boil. Add herbs and let steep for 5-7 minutes.
3. Strain into a cup and add lemon or honey if desired.
4. For the cookies:
5. Preheat oven to 180°C (350°F).
6. In a bowl, mix the spelt flour, sesame seeds, and cinnamon. Add olive oil and honey.
7. Slowly add water and mix until a soft dough forms.
8. Shape into small rounds or ovals and place on a baking sheet lined with parchment.
9. Bake for 12-15 minutes until lightly golden. Let cool before serving.
10. Serve cookies alongside warm tea for a relaxing, balanced snack.

Fat: ~7 g
Carbohydrates: ~18 g
Protein: ~3 g

The values are for 1 single dose

Scientific Background and Health Benefits

This traditional Greek-style snack combines gentle herbs, whole grains, and seeds that promote calmness, digestion, and nourishment.
Herbal teas like mountain tea and chamomile are known for their anti-inflammatory and antioxidant properties, as well as mild calming effects that support better sleep and reduced stress.
Spelt flour is an ancient grain rich in fiber, magnesium, and B vitamins, supporting digestion and energy.
Sesame seeds are a great source of calcium, iron, and healthy fats, all of which support bone density and cardiovascular health.
Olive oil adds heart-healthy fats and aids absorption of fat-soluble nutrients.
This snack is a gentle but functional combination—ideal for winding down or as a light bite between meals.

Senior-Specific Notes
- Easy to chew, especially if cookies are made soft.
- Naturally calming—ideal for afternoon rest or evening routines.
- Supports bone health, digestion, and relaxation.
- Hydrating, with low sugar and balanced nutrients.
- Can be prepared in advance and stored for several days.

Scan the QR to access the bonus: 7-day reset meal plan

Conclusion

Adopting the Mediterranean diet is not just a nutritional choice—it's a lifestyle rooted in tradition, balance, and well-being. For seniors, it offers a powerful path to aging with vitality, clarity, and strength. Through simple, wholesome ingredients and mindful eating, this way of life nourishes the body and uplifts the spirit.

From heart health and cognitive function to improved digestion and lasting energy, the benefits of the Mediterranean diet are especially profound in our later years. But beyond its scientific merits, this diet brings joy back to the table. Whether it's a breakfast of fresh fruit and Greek yogurt or a light, flavorful dinner shared with loved ones, every meal is an opportunity to connect—with food, with culture, and with ourselves.

You now have not only the knowledge of what to eat, but also practical tools—recipes, shopping tips, and daily strategies—to make this way of living your own. Remember, there's no need for perfection. Small, consistent steps lead to meaningful, lasting change.

Embrace the Mediterranean way. Eat well, live well, and celebrate every day with flavor, purpose, and health.

Biography

Bach-Faig, A., Berry, E. M., Lairon, D., Reguant, J., Trichopoulou, A., Dernini, S., Medina, F. X., Battino, M., Belahsen, R., Miranda, G., & Serra-Majem, L. (2011). Mediterranean diet pyramid today. Public Health Nutrition, 14(12A), 2274-2284. https://doi.org/10.1017/S1368980011002515

Davis, C., Bryan, J., Hodgson, J., & Murphy, K. (2015). Definition of the Mediterranean Diet; a Literature Review. Nutrients, 7(11), 9139-9153. https://doi.org/10.3390/nu7115459

Kris-Etherton, P. M., Petersen, K., & Hibbeln, J. R. (2021). Mediterranean Diet and Cognitive Function in Older Adults. Nutrition Today, 56(1), 12-21.

Martínez-González, M. A., & Bes-Rastrollo, M. (2014). Dietary patterns, Mediterranean diet, and cardiovascular disease. Current Opinion in Lipidology, 25(1), 20-26.

Oldways Preservation Trust. (2023). Mediterranean Diet Pyramid. Retrieved from https://oldwayspt.org/traditional-diets/mediterranean-diet

Trichopoulou, A., & Lagiou, P. (2001). Healthy traditional Mediterranean diet: an expression of culture, history, and lifestyle. Public Health Nutrition, 4(4), 943-947.

Willett, W. C., Sacks, F., Trichopoulou, A., Drescher, G., Ferro-Luzzi, A., Helsing, E., & Trichopoulos, D. (1995). Mediterranean diet pyramid: a cultural model for healthy eating. American Journal of Clinical Nutrition, 61(6), 1402S-1406S.

Yannakoulia, M., Kontogianni, M., & Scarmeas, N. (2015). Cognitive health and Mediterranean diet: just diet or lifestyle pattern? Ageing Research Reviews, 20, 74-78.

Estruch, R., Ros, E., Salas-Salvadó, J., et al. (2013). Primary prevention of cardiovascular disease with a Mediterranean diet. New England Journal of Medicine, 368(14), 1279-1290. https://doi.org/10.1056/NEJMoa1200303

Printed in Great Britain
by Amazon